How Does It Grow?

LONDON, NEW YORK, MUNICH, MELBOURNE, and DELHI

First Edition, 2009

Copyright © 2009 Deere & Company.

Published in the United States by DK Publishing
375 Hudson Street, New York, New York 10014

09 10 11 12 13 10 9 8 7 6 5 4 3 2 1

Created and produced by Parachute Publishing, L.L.C.
322 Eighth Avenue, New York, NY 10001

Written by Catherine Nichols
Designed by Michelle Martinez

ISBN 978-0-7566-4447-5

Printed in China

Discover more at
www.dk.com

The publisher would like to thank the following for their kind permission to reproduce their photographs.
ABBREVIATIONS KEY: t-top, b-bottom, r-right, l-left, c-center, a-above, f-far, bkgd-background, bo-border

Cover images
Front Shebeko/Shutterstock.com (tr); Dole/Shutterstock.com (bl); Shutterstock.com (tl)
Back Egidijus Skiparis/Shutterstock.com (tl); Marek Mnich/Shutterstock.com (tr)
Half-title Mirec/Shutterstock.com
Copyright Lezh/Shutterstock.com (tr); photobeps/Shutterstock.com (tr)
Title page Tischenko Irina/Shutterstock.com (tr); Vaclav Mach/Shutterstock.com (br); Dole/Shutterstock.com (bll); Egidijus Skiparis/Shutterstock.com (tl)
4-5 Marko Poplasen/Shutterstock.com (4c); Rafa Irusta/Shutterstock.com (4bll); photobeps/Shutterstock.com (4tr); RoJo Images/Shutterstock.com (4br); Sherry Yates Sowell/Shutterstock.com (5cr); Maksymilian Skolik/Shutterstock.com (5bll); alex7021/Shutterstock.com (5cl); Vaclav Mach/Shutterstock.com (5t); Dole/Shutterstock.com (5br)
6-7 Vaclav Mach/Shutterstock.com (6l); Viktor1/Shutterstock.com (6b); Jeanne Hatch/Shutterstock.com (6tr); Vaclav Mach/Shutterstock.com (7r); JIS/Shutterstock.com (7c)
8-9 Joe Gough/Shutterstock.com (bkgd); Marek Mnich/Shutterstock.com (8c); Stephen Aaron Rees/Shutterstock.com (8br); Igor Dutina/Shutterstock.com (8bo); Adrian Lucki/Shutterstock.com (9br); Wellford Tiller/Shutterstock.com (9c)
10-11 kwest/Shutterstock.com (bkgd); Lezh/Shutterstock.com (10l, 11r); photobeps/Shutterstock.com (10ll); Graca Victoria/Shutterstock.com (10b); Stefanie Mohr Photography/Shutterstock.com (10tr)
12-13 Igor Dutina/Shutterstock.com (12br); Jody Dingle/Shutterstock.com (12c); Fesus Robert/Shutterstock.com (12l); Joe Gough/Shutterstock.com (13b); Danny E Hooks/Shutterstock.com (13bo)
14-15 daruda/Shutterstock.com (bkgd); Stephen Aaron Rees/Shutterstock.com (14tfl, tc); Michael Fritzen/Shutterstock.com (14r); Rafa Irusta/Shutterstock.com (14bll); Alan Levenson/Corbis (15t); Lepas/Shutterstock.com (15fr); igor kisselev/Shutterstock.com (15br)
16-17 Elena Elisseeva/Shutterstock.com (16l); blackjake/iStockphoto.com (16br); Zloneg/Shutterstock.com (17tr)
18-19 Jason Vandehey/Shutterstock.com (18bkgd); Egidijus Skiparis/Shutterstock.com (18tr); Roger Swift/Shutterstock.com (19b); Melissa Brandes/Shutterstock.com (19t)
20-21 Tamara Kulikova/Shutterstock.com (20tr); Dole/Shutterstock.com (20l); Stanislav Mikhalev/Shutterstock.com (20c); Dmitriy Karelin/Shutterstock.com (21bl, br); R. Gino Santa Maria/Shutterstock.com (21bc); Lori Sparkia/Shutterstock.com (21c); Ustyujanin/Shutterstock.com (21fr)
22-23 rgbspace/Shutterstock.com (22bo); O'Jay R. Barbee/Shutterstock.com (22c); Katherine Campbell/Shutterstock.com (22tr); Ragne Kabanova/Shutterstock.com (23br)
24 buket bariskan/Shutterstock.com (bkgd); WitR/Shutterstock.com (24cftl); Lorraine Kourafas/Shutterstock.com (24c); Marcie Fowler - Shining Hope Images/Shutterstock.com (24c); Ljupco Smokovski/Shutterstock.com (24cr); Pinkcandy/Shutterstock.com (24cbl); prawny/iStockphoto.com (24cfl); Cherick/Shutterstock.com (24cbr); Peafactory/Shutterstock.com (24bfr); ultimathule/Shutterstock.com (24ffr); Djordje Zoric/Shutterstock.com (24cfr); Chris P./Shutterstock.com (24cr); JIS/Shutterstock.com (24tr)
Stickers Marko Poplasen/Shutterstock.com (t); Rafa Irusta/Shutterstock.com (c); alex7021/Shutterstock.com (l); Mirec/Shutterstock.com (b); Maksymilian Skolik/Shutterstock.com (cr); photobeps/Shutterstock.com (br)

All other images © Deere & Company.

Every effort has been made to trace the copyright holders of photographs, and we apologize if any omissions have been made.

JOHN DEERE

How Does It Grow?

PARACHUTE PRESS

A Trip to the Farm

Grapes

Look and See

Hi! I'm Johnny Tractor. Come with me to see how plants grow on a farm.

Apples

Carrots

Blueberries

Wheat

Cotton

Corn

Peanuts

Tulips

Growing Tall

Wheat plants grow in fields. The tiny plants look like grass at first. Then they grow taller and taller.

Look and See
Rolls and muffins are made from wheat.

When the wheat turns yellow, it's ready to harvest.
A machine called a combine cuts the wheat.

Rows and Rows of Peanuts

Peanuts grow under the ground, inside shells called pods.

Most pods hold two peanuts, but some hold more or less.

Look and See

Peanuts are ground into paste to make peanut butter.

This tractor is pulling a peanut harvester. The harvester pulls up the plants and picks the peanuts.

On the Vine

Grapes grow on vines. The land where the grapes grow is called a vineyard.

Look and See
Grapes are boiled to make jam and jelly.

Special tractors are used in vineyards.
The tractors are narrow so they can
drive between the rows of grapevines.

Tall Stalks of Corn

A corn plant has a long stalk.
Ears of corn grow on the stalk.

Each ear has
many kernels.

Once the corn grows big and tall, a combine harvests it.

Look and See
These chips are made from corn kernels.

Carrots Down Below

Carrots grow underground. When their orange tops poke through, they are ready to be picked.

This tractor is pulling carrots that have just been picked. The carrots will have to be cleaned and cut before they are ready to eat.

Look and See

You can cook carrots, or you can eat them raw. They taste good both ways.

Trees Full of Apples

Apples grow on trees. An orchard is a place where many fruit trees grow.

Look and See

How is apple juice made? Apples are squeezed until juice dribbles out.

The trees in an orchard are planted in rows. These rows are wide enough for a tractor to drive through.

Blueberry Bushes

Blueberries grow in clusters on bushes. They can be as tiny as a pea or as large as a marble.

Before they ripen, blueberries are green.

Look and See

Blueberries are tasty when baked in pies.

Some people like to go blueberry picking. You don't have to use a machine to do this. All you need is a pail and your fingers!

Flower Power

A tulip is a flower that grows from a bulb.

The tulip plant grows a flower in spring.
Then the bulb stays hidden in the ground.
The next year it will grow and bloom again.

Look and See

Tulips can be cut and made into colorful bouquets.

Picking Cotton

Cotton grows in little clumps called bolls. The bolls are fluffy and full of seeds.

A machine called a cotton picker picks the bolls off the plants.

Look and See

Cotton is used to make cloth. These pieces of cloth will be made into tablecloths.

23

Come and Get It!

Look and See
Can you match each picnic treat with the plant it comes from?

Can you guess why we visited these farms? So we could make this yummy picnic lunch!

Apple Juice

Fresh

24